Published by the Royal Ontario Museum with the generous support
of the Louise Hawley Stone Charitable Trust

Published by the Royal Ontario Museum with the generous support of the Louise Hawley Stone Charitable Trust

Glass Worlds
Paperweights from the ROM's Collection

April 28 to November 25, 2007

Glass paperweights are deceptive. They look very simple,
yet their designs are usually complex—both in pattern and technology.
They are also some of the most complicated glass artifacts to make.
And they appear fragile . . . but in fact are rather solid.
They let the viewer experience a world made of glass.

 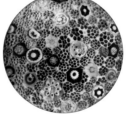 

Glass Worlds

Paperweights from the ROM's Collection

Brian Musselwhite

ROYAL ONTARIO MUSEUM

Royal Ontario Museum
The ROM
100 Queen's Park
Toronto, Ontario
M5S 2C6

www.rom.on.ca

Library and Archives Canada Cataloguing in Publication

Royal Ontario Museum
Glass worlds: paperweights from the ROM's collection / Brian
Musselwhite.
Catalogue of an exhibition held at the Royal Ontario Museum, Toronto, Ont.,
      Apr. 28, 2007–Nov. 25, 2007.
Includes bibliographical references.
ISBN 978-0-88854-449-0
      1. Paperweights--Catalogs. 2. Royal Ontario Museum--Catalogs.
I. Musselwhite, Brian, date II. Title.

NK5440.P3R65 2007   748.8'4   C2007-902006-2

Project Manager: Glen Ellis
Editor: Andrea Gallagher
Designer/Production Coordinator: Virginia Morin
Photographer: Brian Boyle

Printed on acid-free paper by Tri-Graphic Printing, Ottawa, Ontario

Printed and bound in Canada

The Royal Ontario Museum is an agency of the Ontario Ministry of Culture.

Contents

The ROM's Collection of Paperweights   7

Collectors and Collecting   9

Historical Summary: Paperweights Through Time   11

What is a Paperweight?   12

Writing, Reading, and Desks   14

Description of Paperweights   17

Unusual Types of Paperweights   25

Early Classic French Paperweights 1845–1855   33

Early North American Paperweights 1850–1935   57

English and Scottish Paperweights 1845–1960   77

Central and Northern European Paperweights,

    Chinese Paperweights, 1845–1970   87

Recent North American Paperweights 1950–Present   95

Bibliography   119

See page 13.

The ROM's Collection of Paperweights

A relatively recent creation, the paperweight collection at the Royal Ontario Museum has quickly become one of the most important in the world. It ranks among the four finest public collections in North America. Credit for this is largely due to the generosity of two donors and their families. All of the paperweights and glass illustrated in this book and displayed in the accompanying exhibition are part of the collection of the Royal Ontario Museum.

The ROM had few paperweights until 1981 when the substantial collection of Mrs. Alice Baldwin Hall was donated. Although Mrs. Hall specialized in French paperweights of the Classic period of the mid-19th century, she also had significant mid-20th-century examples of the works of Charles Kaziun (1919–1992) and Paul Ysart (1904–1991) as well as numerous contemporary paperweights by unknown artists from around the world. Her collection of 281 paperweights plus related materials is all the more amazing when one realizes that when she was collecting there were very few books on the subject and most of those were unreliable.

J. A. Howson "Brock" Brocklebank and his wife, Millie, also collected glass paperweights. They knew of the Hall collection and felt that they could not compete. Fortuitously for the Museum, therefore, they decided to focus on contemporary American paperweight-makers. They delighted in meeting artists such as Paul Stankard (b. 1943) and Rick Ayotte (b. 1944) and never failed to purchase major examples of their work. In 1984, the J. A. Howson Brocklebank estate gave to the ROM a fine collection of 135 modern American paperweights. To ensure that the collection would continue to grow, "Brock" also left to the Museum the J. A. Howson Brocklebank Fund, which allows curatorial staff to purchase important paperweights for the collection on an ongoing basis. The fund also sustains the Annual Brocklebank ROM-Life Program, permitting lectures by glass paperweight artists, authors, dealers, researchers, and collectors.

The ROM wishes also to thank Mark Armstrong, Dr. Peter Kaellgren, Thomas B. King, Dr. Lorne Pierce, David Roberts, Ms. Nancy Shanoff, Mrs. R. H. Shepherd, Arthur Smith, Edith Chown Pierce and Gerald Stevens, John and Mary Yaremko, and all of the other donors who have shared their love of glass paperweights with visitors to the Museum.

For support and assistance in preparing this catalogue, the author would like to thank Conrad Biernacki, Brian Boyle, Glen Ellis, Andrea Gallagher, Dr. Peter Kaellgren, Richard Lahey, Deb Metsger, Virginia Morin, Barb Rice, Catherine Wyss, the members of the ROM Art & Archaeology Editorial Board, and the Louise Hawley Stone Charitable Trust.

In memory of my parents, Allan and May Musselwhite

Collectors and Collecting

Past generations were mesmerized by paperweights and formed important collections. The early-20th-century French writer Colette was so proud of her "small frozen gardens" that she was photographed with them.[1] Among European royals in the mid-19th century, Empress Eugénie, the wife of the Emperor Napoleon III of France, collected paperweights, as did Empress Carlotta, the wife of the Emperor Maximilian of Mexico. The Duke of Cardoza, the Princess Murat, and the Marquis of Bailleul also assembled notable collections.[2]

During the 20th century, one of the most famous collectors of paperweights was King Farouk of Egypt. After his abdication in 1952, his large collection of 350 paperweights became one of the first to be publicly auctioned.

It was soon followed by the 1953 Sotheby's sale in London of the important Applewhaite-Abbott Collection, which ushered in a renewed interest in collecting paperweights. The Sotheby's 1957 sale of the Maurice Lindon collection brought out more collectors. Even the seller was inspired to resume his collection of paperweights. Paul Jokelson, founder of the Paperweight Collectors' Association, sold 71 of his finest paperweights in a record-breaking sale at Sotheby's in 1983.[3]

---

1 See Gérard Ingold, *The Art of the Paperweight: Saint Louis* (Santa Cruz, CA: Paperweight Press, 1981), 14.

2 See Paul Hollister, Jr., *The Encyclopedia of Glass Paperweights* (New York: Bramhall House, 1969), 2.

3 See Lawrence H. Selman, *The Art of the Paperweight* (Santa Cruz, CA: Paperweight Press, 1988), 194.

One of the paperweights most sought after today is the rare French salamander from the Cristallerie de Pantin (suburb of Paris). Salamanders were thought to live in fire, possibly because they were sometimes seen crawling out of damp wood when it was added to the fire. The salamander was therefore adopted as the symbol of glassmakers who made their living by fire—and it later became the symbol of firefighters, too. A modern interpretation of the salamander by Victor Trabucco (b. 1949) is shown on page 109.

Historical Summary: Paperweights Through Time

Paperweights quickly became luxury items that satisfied the Victorian taste for ornamentation while serving the important function of keeping papers organized in drafty rooms. These small glass "jewels" became fashionable during a time when education grew in importance for the upper and middle classes, and when the popular activity of letter-writing was at its height.

The pre-eminent period of paperweight-making occurred in France between 1845 and 1855 in the towns of Baccarat, Saint-Louis, and Clichy. These years are known as the Classic period. While the Bacchus factory in England produced paperweights during this period also, in general, production of paperweights in England and the United States began slightly later.

The art of paperweight-making declined from 1900 to 1940, but a "renaissance" occurred in the 1940s and 1950s with Paul Ysart in Scotland and Charles Kaziun in the United States leading the way.

Today the number of paperweight artists is growing. The development of smaller melting devices—burners using compressed gas and oxygen—has allowed glassmakers to work independently, pursuing their own unique talents.

What is a Paperweight?

Paperweights with a few important exceptions are solid glass. They feature a clear glass dome with decorative elements made of glass inside. First appearing in early Victorian times, they are a fairly recent development in the history of glassmaking.

While the primary materials and components were known and made in the ancient world, the technology of paperweight-making was discovered only in the 19th century. Scrambled cane paperweights exhibited at international exhibitions by the Italian glass artist Pietro Bigaglia (1786–1876) sparked an interest in various countries about this new type of object. Bigaglia's company won a gold medal at the Exhibition of Austrian Industry in Vienna in 1845. Not all of his paperweights were of award-winning quality. He also produced ordinary commercial paperweights with small scrambled pieces of filigree. None of his paperweights had a thick dome of glass.

It was in France, sometime in the early 1840s, that an unknown French glassmaker first put a clear glass dome over canes or flamework to create the first glass paperweights as we know them today. Significantly, the simple addition of a glass dome magnified the underlying flamework or canework, allowing the viewer to experience a world made of glass.

Scrambled Cane Paperweight with Knob

Italian, Venetian, Pietro Bigaglia (1786–1876), 1843–1847
D 7.7 cm, H 5.1 cm

Scrambled sections of canes including white and yellow twisted filigree *vetro a retorti*
and thicker red and white, blue and white, and green and white twisted canes;
remains of pontil mark.

Gift of Alice Baldwin Hall. Certified by the Canadian Cultural Property Export
Review Board under the terms of the Cultural Property Export and Import Act.

981.19.135

Writing, Reading, and Desks

For centuries, letter-writing was the only means of long-distance communication and continued to be so for most of the 19th century. During this time, as education became more important and widespread among the upper and middle classes, the numbers of people who could read and write increased. Advice for the newly literate expounding the virtues of good letter-writing and good penmanship could be found in numerous books on deportment. One such guide, in a chapter entitled "The Art of Letter Writing," gave the following advice:

> The writing [of] a note or letter, the wording of a regret, the prompt or the delayed answering of an invitation, the manner of a salutation, the neglect of a required attention, all betray to the well-bred the degree or the absence of good-breeding.
>
> A person who has self-respect as well as respect for others, should never carelessly write a letter or note.[1]

In England, the Post Office Reform pamphlet of 1837 by Rowland Hill promoted a prepaid uniform rate of postage by weight. This was accepted by

---

1 John H. Young, *Our Deportment or the Manners, Conduct and Dress of the Most Refined Society; Including Forms for Letters, Invitations, Etc., Etc. Also, Valuable Suggestions on Home Culture and Training* (Detroit and St. Louis: F. B. Dickerson & Co., rev. ed., 1882), chapter 22.

Parliament on January 10, 1840, and the first adhesive postage stamp, the Penny Black, was issued for use on May 6, 1840.[1] Queen Victoria's profile on this stamp was the inspiration for the sulphide paperweight (see Sulphide Paperweight, page 27).

Paperweights emerged in tandem with popular literacy and as men and women had to spend a certain amount of time at their tables or desks, glass factories were happy to supply all of the desk paraphernalia to accompany ink and paper. Glass pens, glass nib wipes, glass seals, and glass straight edges were other accessories made by the glass factories.

Before electric lights became available in the late 1800s, desks and writing tables were placed in front of windows to receive as much daylight as possible. And when the windows were opened, papers on the desk would start to rustle with the breezes. They needed to be weighted down.

The hazard of a draft from an open window is the usual reason noted for the birth of the glass paperweight, although in light of the total clutter on a typical Victorian desk, surely there were many other objects that could have been used for the purpose. Most likely, as the Victorians spent so much time at their desks, they just wanted to look at something beautiful.

----

1 See R. F. Schoolley-West, *Stamps* (London: British Library, 1987), 5–6.

Seal with Bouquet of Flowers (Strawflowers?) Paperweight

Possibly Russian or Bohemian, made for the Russian market, 1850s
D 4.3 cm, H of paperweight 2.4 cm, L of seal 6.6 cm

Central pink flamework flower with yellow centre, surrounded by five flamework flowers in
pink, yellow and pink, peach, mauve, and blue, separated by bright blue and green leaves; cut with
six panels and a top hexagonal window; set upon a panelled shaft; engraved on seal
with an interlocking "DI."

This acquisition was made possible with the generous support of
the J. A. Howson Brocklebank Fund.

988.228.1

Description of Paperweights

Paperweights are classified by size as well as decoration.

Size

Abbreviations for dimensions of the paperweights in this book are D (diameter), H (height), L (length), and W (width). There are three standard traditional sizes:

Miniature—any paperweight less than 5 cm (2 in.) in diameter.

Common—any paperweight about 7 cm (2¾ in.) in diameter.

Magnum—any paperweight more than 8.5 cm (3⅜ in.) in diameter.

Decoration

Experts use a special vocabulary to describe and identify paperweights.

Cane—a prepared rod of glass with either glass spiralling "threads" on its surface (see **Filigree**) or an enclosed pattern running its full length and visible only when seen in cross-section. Rods must be reduced to a size suitable for a paperweight. The process begins at the furnace: a glassmaker dips the end of his pontil rod (see **Pontil**) into a tank of molten glass and collects a gather of glass. An assistant attaches a second pontil rod to the opposite end of the gather. They both draw it (pull it) out in opposite directions, thereby reducing its diameter to the required size. The drawn-out rods are then cooled (annealled) and broken into sections. At this point, with direct heat, these rods can be manipulated to form flowers or figures (see **Flamework**).

To make a simple millefiori cane (see **Millefiori**), the drawn-out coloured glass rods are bundled into the required pattern. The bundled canes are re-heated and attached to a pontil rod with a gather. A second pontil rod is again attached and the bundle is drawn out, reducing the diameter of the bundle without destroying the internal pattern. The resulting millefiori cane is cooled and broken into short manageable lengths, which are arranged with others to create the paperweight design. This is then heated and covered with a colourless glass dome and base.

Canework—decoration using cane sections. Canework began with simple canes as decorative additions on ancient Egyptian perfume containers, but really flourished under the Roman Empire. Made for the wealthy, small millefiori bowls, gaming pieces, and highly decorative slices of caned floral inlay for furniture have survived to show later generations the high level of excellence that the Roman glassmakers achieved with this art. After the fall of Rome, the art was rediscovered in the late 15th century by the Renaissance glassmakers of Venice and Murano, who used canework as a staple for objects such as drinking glasses and footed dishes. These in turn inspired the glassmakers of the Netherlands to produce elaborate canework stems on tall drinking glasses. The Dutch glassmakers could only approximate the Murano canes as their glass was made with a potash flux (see **Flux**) rather than a soda flux, which was used by the Venetians and the Romans.

By the 1760s the English took up the challenge and used mostly white twisted filigree canes to great effect in their drinking-glass stems.

It was the French factory of Baccarat, however, that was most prolific in producing large objects such as jugs and carafes made entirely of canes. Thin slices of spaced millefiori canes giving the appearance of so many scattered flowers were used in clear glass decanters, glasses, carafes, and trays. The impression of a flower garden was further enhanced with wheel-engraved and gilded stems and leaves.

Italian glassmakers continued to make the cane a staple for much of their decoration, producing many decorative objects for the tastes of late-19th-century consumers. As the styles changed, the cane proved to be perfectly suited to Art Nouveau, Art Deco, and Art Moderne, culminating in one of the 20th century's most enduring icons of modern design, the *fazzoletto* or handkerchief vase, which was introduced in 1949 by Fulvio Bianconi (1915–1996) and Paolo Venini (1895–1959).

American paperweight-maker Richard Marquis (b. 1945) is one of the contemporary artists who has embraced the cane. His "found" objects such as his combined glass teapot–drinking glass under a glass dome are not only made of canes but also have numerous applied cane slices. In Canada, Virginia Wilson Toccalino (b. 1955) and her husband Tony Toccalino (b. 1952) incorporate canes in their paperweights as well as in larger objects.

Carpet ground—tightly packed millefiori canes set randomly or in concentric circles, producing a consistent pattern or colour and giving the appearance of a carpet.

Chequer or barber's pole—white twisted filigree segments set in a chequerboard pattern around spaced canes. Twisted filigree segments that include red and green or more often blue with the white canes are called "barber's pole" because they look like striped barber's poles.

Crimp—a rose-shaped metal tool used to push a glob of coloured glass up into the clear glass, to make a flower or other object.

Cut-base—base of paperweight with wheel-cut decoration. The most common cut-base decorations are stars (hence, star-cut base) or "strawberry diamond" cutting (a fine chequerboard pattern).

Faceting—a method of decorating whereby an abrasive wheel removes circular or oval slices from the glass dome of the paperweight, leaving flat or slightly concave facets, called printies (see **Printies**). Larger facets on overlays (see **Overlay**) are called windows.

Filigree—a colourless glass rod within white or coloured spiralling glass threads.

Flashing—a thin layer of translucent coloured glass.

Flamework (formerly called lampwork)—the creation of realistic three-dimensional objects by manipulating melted glass rods over a flame. Its origins date back to at least 500 BCE. Phoenician glassmakers from the eastern end of the Mediterranean Sea made small glass human heads, possibly for use as jewellery. Diminutive vases and perfume containers were also formed by this method.

Flamework died out with the fall of Rome and almost vanished during the Middle Ages, but it reappeared as a flourishing industry in Nevers, France, in the 1600s. Large complex groups of glass figures in the form of gods and goddesses were fashioned for the dessert table while other groups relating to the Bible were used for private devotion. Many of the figures were made by members of the Saroldi family, glassmakers from the Italian town of Altare, who came to France with Ludovico Gonzaga, later Duke of Nevers, when he married Henrietta of Cleves.

By the mid-1800s, British glassmakers embraced flamework and were producing unbelievable confections protected by glass domes.

Examples from the 20th century include those hundreds of thousands of glass animals produced by numerous glass artists, at fairs and street corners, and whose work was memorialized by American playwright Tennessee Williams in *The Glass Menagerie*.

Canadian 20th-century examples include the 1960s flamework of

Elmore Hookway (1889–1974) and the perfume bottles by Alexander Kapran (1954–2006). Both these artists are worthy successors to the glassmakers of Nevers.

Flux—a chemical compound used to lower the melting point of silica (sand, which is about 75 per cent of the composition of glass) from about 1850°C to about 1300°C, an easier temperature to maintain. The flux can be soda (sodium carbonate), as used by the Venetians; potash (potassium carbonate), as used by the northern Europeans; or lead oxide, which was introduced in England by George Ravenscroft about 1676.

Millefiori (Italian, meaning "thousand flowers")—decoration consisting of cross-sections of bundled solid glass rods (canes) placed together to create the impression of a field or carpet of flowers.

Muslin—white scrambled (see **Scrambled**) filigree canes that together resemble the white cotton fabric.

Overlay—a paperweight encased within one or more thin outer layers of glass (thicker than flashing and usually opaque), then cut with printies or windows to reveal the inside.

Pontil (also called the "puntee" or "punty")—the long solid iron rod onto which a partially made molten glass object is transferred. When the object is finished and removed from the rod, a rough pontil mark remains.

Pontil mark—the rough mark at the centre of the bottom of a paperweight or other blown-glass object where the pontil was attached while the object was being created. The mark can be smoothed out by reheating the glass surface or by grinding it after the object has been cooled (annealled) to room temperature.

Printie—circular or oval facet or window, several of which may be cut into the sides of the glass dome of a paperweight.

Scrambled—haphazard, in reference to the arrangement of short broken sections of glass canes.

Torsade—a ring of twisted opaque white or coloured glass encircling a mushroom or upright bouquet.

Vetro a retorti—glass with embedded canes that form various spiral patterns.

See page 31.

Unusual Types of Paperweights

By definition, paperweights are made entirely of glass: the extreme high temperature of molten glass destroys everything else. Yet, there are three main exceptions to the rule, which all derive from earlier decorative forms (of the same name) that were later applied to paperweight manufacturing.

Sulphides are white porcelainous ceramic cameos encased in glass. The name is deceiving as this white ceramic did not contain sulphur. Red sulphur cameos, also called sulphides or sulphurs, were produced for collectors in the 18th century, however, and they were probably the source of the name for the 18th-century white plaster cameos.

White porcelainous cameos first appeared in Bohemia in the 1750s. The finest portrait medallions made between 1769 and 1791 in Scotland by James Tassie (1735–1799) are not related, however, as his examples were made with a "vitreous white paste" melted into mounds. The evolution of the sulphide continued with a Frenchman, Barthélémy Desprez (act. about 1815–1834), who was the first to encapsulate cameos in transparent glass—in effect creating proto-paperweights. Pierre Honoré Boudon de Saint-Annas (1774–1858) improved the art and received the first patent in 1818.

In England, Apsley Pellatt (1791–1863) at his Falcon Glassworks in Southwark, London, saw the possibilities for these "glass incrustations" or "crystallo ceramie" and obtained a patent for his process in 1819. The material memorialized famous people of the day. Pellatt published a book in which he included illustrations of two glass obelisks that could be used to "press paper."[1] By the 1850s, paperweight-makers were incorporating similar cameos into their products. The French companies of Baccarat and Saint-Louis continue to make sulphides today.

Enamelled gold-foil medallions of floral bouquets or tiny replicas of medals such as the French Legion of Honour were first encapsulated in the walls of tumblers before they appeared in paperweights. Canadian John Gooderham (1930–2007) was a master of this technique.

Pinchbecks are named after Christopher Pinchbeck (1670–1732), a London watch- and clockmaker who invented the metallic alloy that resembles gold and was used in making inexpensive jewellery. Pinchbeck paperweights look like traditional paperweights but are not made of solid glass. They are made up of three components: a metallic-alloy panel pressed with a scene in high relief, which is placed in a porcelain mount, then topped by a separate solid clear glass dome. As the materials are glued together and not fused, they were not made in glass factories.

---

1 Apsley Pellatt, *Memoir on the Origin, Progress, and Improvement of Glass Manufactures: Including an Account of the Patent Crystallo Ceramie, or, Glass Incrustations* (London: B. J. Holdsworth, 1821), figs. 19, 24.

Sulphide Paperweight

French, Clichy, 1845–1855
D 7.3 cm, H 5.1 cm

Encapsulated sulphide bust profile portrait of the young Queen Victoria wearing her crown, encircled with a ring of five bright blue canes alternating with groups of three smaller white canes; on a suspended bright red ground; five circular printies with five deep vertical flutes and a large top printie.

This acquisition was made possible with the generous support of the J. A. Howson Brocklebank Fund.

987.279.3

Sulphide Paperweight

Possibly French, Baccarat, 1845–1855
D 6.6 cm, H 4.7 cm

Encapsulated sulphide of the Immaculate Conception with the Virgin standing on a
crescent moon supported by clouds with four cherubs, possibly after a painting by
the Spanish artist Bartolomé Esteban Murillo (1617–1682).

Gift of Alice Baldwin Hall. Certified by the Canadian Cultural Property Export
Review Board under the terms of the Cultural Property Export and Import Act.
981.19.59

Sulphide Paperweight

Probably English, 1851
D 7.4 cm, H 5 cm

Encapsulated oval sulphide showing the 1851 "Crystal Palace"[1] with the words filled in with teal blue: "BUILDING FOR THE GREAT EXHIBITION OF INDUSTRY OF ALL NATIONS IN LONDON 1851."

Gift of Mrs. R. H. Shepherd

977.92

---

1 The Crystal Palace, designed by Joseph Paxton (1803–1865) and built in Hyde Park, London, for the Great Exhibition of 1851, was the first great exhibition building of prefabricated glass and cast iron. After the exhibition, the building was moved to Sydenham, a suburb of London, where it was enlarged. It was destroyed by fire in 1936.

Sulphide Paperweight

French, Baccarat, Gilbert Poillerat (1902–1988), 1953
D 7.1 cm, H 3.8 cm

Encapsulated sulphide bust profile portraits of Queen Elizabeth II and Prince Philip, Duke of Edinburgh, on a deep blue ground with six side printies and one top printie; impressed on edge of sulphide: "G. POILLERAT"; acid-etched on side of base: "BACCARAT 1953." Made to commemorate the coronation of Elizabeth II.

Gift of Alice Baldwin Hall. Certified by the Canadian Cultural Property Export Review Board under the terms of the Cultural Property Export and Import Act.
981.19.67

Pinchbeck

French, 1850s

D 8.1 cm, H 4.7 cm

A circular thin moulded metal-alloy panel in a matte finish with some burnishing for highlights, showing Leda and the Swan, by a lake in a garden with four water nymphs and a hovering Cupid with his bow; set in a white porcelain mount and finished with a separate dome of glass.

This acquisition was made possible with the generous support of the J. A. Howson Brocklebank Fund.

987.279.2

See page 41.

Early Classic French Paperweights 1845–1855

In the early 1840s, the French glass houses produced the first glass paperweights as we know them today—a design set low, fused under a clear magnifying dome.

While Baccarat, Saint-Louis, and Clichy made paperweights superficially similar in appearance, each factory used distinctive canes and different formulas for the clear glass dome, which today help in identifying the originating factory. Occasionally, paperweights contained dated canes.

Baccarat

The Compagnie des Cristalleries de Baccarat, Baccarat (in northeastern France, southeast of Nancy), has been active since 1764. Baccarat specialized in flamework flowers, carpet-ground paperweights (tightly packed canes), silhouette canes, garlands, snakes, and butterflies hovering over a flower. The company continues to make paperweights today.

Saint-Louis

The Compagnie des Cristalleries de Saint-Louis, Saint-Louis (near Bitche in northeastern France), made some of the first paperweights. It has been active since 1767. Saint-Louis specialized in mushroom paperweights (in which the canes rise up to form a mushroom shape) and flowers or fruit set above spiralling canes. Saint-Louis continues to make paperweights today.

Clichy

The glass factory of L. Joseph Maës, Clichy-la-Garenne (now a suburb north of Paris on the Seine River near Montmartre), was active from about 1837 to 1885. Clichy had its green-edged pink "rose" cane and specialized in canes set on "muslin" (white scrambled canes), barber's poles (blue and white canes), swirls, caned "baskets," and garlands.

The "Clichy rose" was not exclusive to Clichy. It was originally made by the Italian glassmakers Giovanni Battista Franchini (1804–1873) and his son Giacomo (1827–1897), but because the Clichy glassmakers used it so often, Clichy has always received the credit for inventing it.[1]

1 See Jutta-Annette Bruhn, *Designs in Miniature: The Story of Mosaic Glass* (Corning, NY: Corning Museum of Glass, 1995), 30.

Baccarat

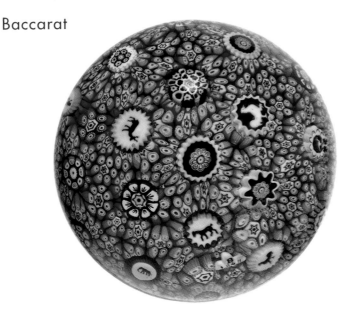

Red "Carpet" Ground

French, Baccarat, 1848
D 7.8 cm, H 5.2 cm

Red and white millefiori canes with concentric rings around spaced canes, including silhouettes of animals and birds and a date cane with "B 1848."

Gift of Alice Baldwin Hall. Certified by the Canadian Cultural Property Export Review Board under the terms of the Cultural Property Export and Import Act.

981.19.39

Faceted Mushroom with Torsade

French, Baccarat, 1845–1855
D 8.1 cm, H 5.7 cm

Close millefiori canes, encircled with a blue and white spiral torsade, faceted with three rows of ten interlocking pentagons and hexagons; star-cut base.

Gift of Alice Baldwin Hall. Certified by the Canadian Cultural Property Export Review Board under the terms of the Cultural Property Export and Import Act.

981.19.40

Clematis

French, Baccarat, 1845-1855
D 8 cm, H 5.3 cm

Overlapping blue ribbed flamework petals with central white star, red-lined, within a
yellow cane with transparent stars, a smaller blue ribbed clematis with central blue and white
cane, green stem, and seven leaves; encircled with a band of alternating canes (red and
white canes alternate with red, green, and white canes); two rows of circular concave
printies, those in the lower row larger, and a large top printie; star-cut base.

Gift of Alice Baldwin Hall. Certified by the Canadian Cultural Property Export
Review Board under the terms of the Cultural Property Export and Import Act.

981.19.62

Purple Dahlia

French, Baccarat, 1845-1855
D 7.1 cm, H 4.6 cm

Purple and mauve striped multi-layered flamework petals with a red centre surrounded
by white star canes, with a green stem and nine green leaves; star-cut base.

Gift of Alice Baldwin Hall. Certified by the Canadian Cultural Property Export Review
Board under the terms of the Cultural Property Export and Import Act.

981.19.54

Rose

French, Baccarat, 1845–1855
D 6.8 cm, H 4.4 cm

Red "thousand-petalled" flamework rose with green stem and twelve leaves.

Gift of Alice Baldwin Hall. Certified by the Canadian Cultural Property Export
Review Board under the terms of the Cultural Property Export and Import Act.
981.19.52

Pink Snake on White Muslin

French, Baccarat, 1845-1855
D 8 cm, H 5.8 cm

Mottled pink and brown spiral flamework snake on a white scrambled filigree ground.

Gift of Alice Baldwin Hall. Certified by the Canadian Cultural Property Export
Review Board under the terms of the Cultural Property Export and Import Act.

981.19.63

Butterfly over Flower

French, Baccarat, 1845–1855
D 7.6 cm, H 4.8 cm

Multi-coloured flamework butterfly hovering over a white ribbed double-layered clematis with a central red- and white-ringed cane surrounded by a cluster of white star canes; green stem and thirteen green leaves; star-cut base.

Gift of Alice Baldwin Hall. Certified by the Canadian Cultural Property Export Review Board under the terms of the Cultural Property Export and Import Act.

981.19.60

Saint-Louis

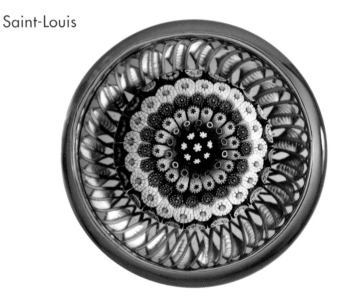

Mushroom with Torsade

French, Saint-Louis, 1848
D 7.7 cm, H 5.2 cm

Millefiori mushroom with a central star cluster surrounded by five concentric rings, predominately blue, white, and green, the outer ring with a date cane: "SL1848"; encircled with a pink and white spiral torsade; star-cut base.

981.19.89

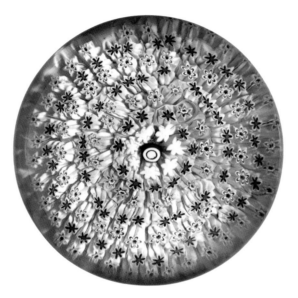

Concentric

French, Saint-Louis, 1845–1855
D 7.8 cm, H 4.9 cm

A large red- and white-ringed central cane within a star cluster, surrounded by six concentric rings, with rings of blue- and pink-centred canes alternating with rings of blue-centred canes; set onto an opaque yellow-green ground.

Gift of Alice Baldwin Hall. Certified by the Canadian Cultural Property Export Review Board under the terms of the Cultural Property Export and Import Act.

981.19.32

Concentric

French, Saint-Louis, 1845–1855
D 7.6 cm, H 5.1 cm

A central white profile of a man, possibly the puppet Punch or François I, King of France
(r. 1515–1547), surrounded by five concentric rings including a ring of the white
"dancing devil" in a lime-lined cane.

Gift of Alice Baldwin Hall. Certified by the Canadian Cultural Property Export
Review Board under the terms of the Cultural Property Export and Import Act.

981.19.80

Pansy and Chamomile

French, Saint-Louis, 1845–1855
D 7.3 cm, H 5.6 cm

Orange and purple flamework pansy and a white multi-petalled chamomile with green stem, five leaves, and a bud, encircled with a ring of alternating canes (white and rose canes alternate with green, rose, and white canes); faceted in ten panels of four rows, with a top central window.

Gift of Alice Baldwin Hall. Certified by the Canadian Cultural Property Export Review Board under the terms of the Cultural Property Export and Import Act.

981.19.74

Bouquet

French, Saint-Louis, 1845–1855
D 7.8 cm, H 5.3 cm

Flamework bouquet with large central ribbed pink flower with large central air bubble
over a central white cane, surrounded by a blue ribbed and a white ribbed smaller
flower and two different blue and white millefiori canes set on numerous leaves;
in a double-spiral white filigree *vetro a retorti* basket with a red and white
filigree handle finished with a rose-edged millefiori cane.

Gift of Alice Baldwin Hall. Certified by the Canadian Cultural Property Export
Review Board under the terms of the Cultural Property Export and Import Act.
981.19.70

Vegetables

French, Saint-Louis, 1845–1855
D 7.8 cm, H 5.6 cm

Flamework carrot, radish, and turnips set on a double-spiral white filigree
vetro a retorti ground.

This acquisition was made possible with the generous support of
the J. A. Howson Brocklebank Fund.

987.52.3

Fruit

French, Saint-Louis, 1845–1855
D 7.3 cm, H 4.7 cm

Flamework apple or peach, a yellow and an amber pear, and four red cherries with stems and
assorted green leaves; set on a double-swirl white filigree *vetro a retorti* basket.

Gift of Alice Baldwin Hall. Certified by the Canadian Cultural Property Export
Review Board under the terms of the Cultural Property Export and Import Act.

981.19.79

Clichy

Miniature Paperweight

French, Clichy, 1845–1855
D 4.6 cm, H 3.5 cm

Scrambled canes including a cane with separate white rods with pale blue letters spelling "CLICHY."

This acquisition was made possible with the generous support of the J. A. Howson Brocklebank Fund.

988.231.1

Barber's Pole

French, Clichy, 1845–1855
D 8.1 cm, H 5.3 cm

Two concentric rings of spaced millefiori canes including a "Clichy rose" surrounding a large white cane with green and pink center, separated with short lengths of blue and white filigree twists suspended above parallel sections of various white filigree twists."

Gift of Alice Baldwin Hall. Certified by the Canadian Cultural Property Export Review Board under the terms of the Cultural Property Export and Import Act.

981.19.21

Millefiori

French, Clichy, 1845–1855
D 8.2 cm, H 5.2 cm

Close millefiori canes including numerous "Clichy roses" with alternating
deep blue and white stave sides.

Gift of Alice Baldwin Hall. Certified by the Canadian Cultural Property Export
Review Board under the terms of the Cultural Property Export and Import Act.

981.19.2

51

Mushroom

French, Clichy, 1845–1855
D 7 cm, H 4.7 cm

Close millefiori canes including a "Clichy rose," with alternating pink and white stave sides, six large circular printies, and one large top printie; star-cut base.

Gift of Alice Baldwin Hall. Certified by the Canadian Cultural Property Export Review Board under the terms of the Cultural Property Export and Import Act.

981.19.1

Pedestal

French, Clichy, 1845–1855
D 7.3 cm, H 6.3 cm

Eight concentric rings of millefiori canes including a central "Clichy rose"
and seven surrounding "Clichy roses," set on alternating white and
lime-green spiralling stave sides.

Gift of Alice Baldwin Hall. Certified by the Canadian Cultural Property Export
Review Board under the terms of the Cultural Property Export and Import Act.
981.19.169

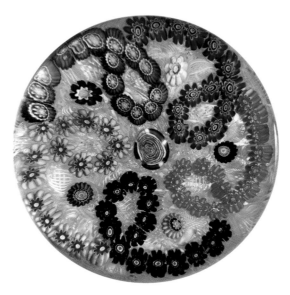

Garlands on White Muslin

French, Clichy, 1845–1855
D 7.8 cm, H 6 cm

Interlocking pink, green, deep red, turquoise, and purple garlands spaced with individual canes surrounding a central "Clichy rose," set on scrambled filigree twists suspended above parallel sections of various white filigree twists.

Gift of Alice Baldwin Hall. Certified by the Canadian Cultural Property Export Review Board under the terms of the Cultural Property Export and Import Act.

981.19.16

Swirl

French, Clichy, 1845–1855
D 7.7 cm, H 5.2 cm

Swirled alternating white and lime-green stripes, from a central white and
green cane surrounded by a cluster of white star canes.

Gift of Alice Baldwin Hall. Certified by the Canadian Cultural Property Export
Review Board under the terms of the Cultural Property Export and Import Act.
981.19.8

See page 63.

Early North American Paperweights 1850–1935

United States

The first American paperweights in the 1850s were pressed—not surprising, since the Americans had invented and perfected the glass-pressing machine in the 1820s. For the other glass products, the developing glass factories, started by European immigrants of French or English ancestry, needed skilled workers and were continually enticing European glassworkers to work in New England.

The first millefiori and flamework paperweights produced in the 1850s in these factories look French—again not surprising, since a number of these immigrants had apprenticed at Baccarat and Saint-Louis. Some American paperweights were distinctly original, however. These included the large roses produced by the Mount Washington Glass Company of New Bedford, Massachusetts, in the 1870s and the apple or pear paperweights produced by the New England Glass Company, which were finer than the French originals. Unfortunately, little is known about most of the paperweight-makers at any of these factories, the exceptions being Nicolas (1838–1904) and François (Frank) Lutz (1832–1874), who both apprenticed at Saint-Louis. Head gaffer at the Boston & Sandwich Glass Company by day, Nicolas made flamework fruit and flowers for paperweights in his basement in his home at night. These simple designs were then made into paperweights by his shop.[1]

---

[1] See John D. Hawley, *The Art of the Paperweight: The Boston & Sandwich and New England Glass Companies* (Santa Cruz, CA: Paperweight Press, 1997).

At the World's Columbian Exposition in Chicago, Illinois, in 1893, the Libbey Glass Company displayed a complete working glass factory. Visitors could purchase simple moulded glass paperweights with a chromolithograph (coloured paper print) of the factory glued to the underside. They could also purchase other paperweights at the fair, some dated with the year 1892 and some with the year 1893. The confusion occurred because the fair was supposed to celebrate the 400th anniversary of Christopher Columbus's landing in the New World, hence 1892. But the organization of the fair took longer than anticipated and it did not open until 1893.

From the 1890s to the 1930s, elaborate paperweights were rarely produced, probably because of the introduction of machines such as the Owens Automatic Gathering and Blowing Machine (see Promotional Paperweight, page 65) in the 1890s in glass factories across North America. The machines effectively ended the careers of many glassworkers, without whom the traditional hand-worked paperweights could not be made, accounting for their scarcity during this period.

Machines, however, did not do away with the paperweight; it was reinvented in the form of a moulded-glass block. These blocks were ideally suited for promotional advertising or for showing off family photographs or local attractions.

Canada

Canada had no tradition of creating elaborate paperweights in the 19th century. Its population was too small to support large glass factories with their large skilled work forces. In addition, Canada imported much of its glassware from Great Britain and the United States, so there was less of an incentive to open a glass factory.

The majority of the glass factories that opened in the 19th century closed within ten to fifteen years. And most of those could make a living only by producing functional objects such as bottles or simple wares for the table. Only after 1879, when the government imposed heavy tariffs of 30 per cent of the value of imported pressed glassware, was there a reason to start a glass factory.[1]

But these were not the sort of factories that could produce elaborate paperweights because, like their American counterparts at this time, some of them also imported the Owens Automatic Gathering and Blowing Machine. When the Hamilton Glass Company–Diamond Glass Co. Ltd. was rebuilt in 1906, for instance, it had two of the Owens automatic machines.[2]

---

1 See Janet Holmes, *Patterns in Light: The John and Mary Yaremko Glass Collection* (Toronto: Royal Ontario Museum, 1987), 7.
2 See Gerald Stevens, *Canadian Glass, c. 1825-1925* (Toronto: Ryerson Press, 1967), 9-11.

Canadians also enthusiastically accepted the reinvented paperweight form. Machine-made paperweights were used for promotional advertising or to show off family photographs or local attractions. As today, however, not all paperweights relating to Canada were made in Canada; many were produced in the United States or other countries.

Cross, Two Anchors, and a Leaf

American, Boston & Sandwich Glass Company, Sandwich, Massachusetts, 1852–1880
D 6.8 cm, H 4.6 cm

Red flamework cross with central cane, with two anchors angling from the cross,
all with mauve detailing; a red- and mauve-striped leaf below.

Gift of Alice Baldwin Hall. Certified by the Canadian Cultural Property Export
Review Board under the terms of the Cultural Property Export and Import Act.
989.256.17

Pear on a "Cookie"

American, New England Glass Company, East Cambridge, Massachusetts, 1860–1880
D of "cookie" 6.8 cm, H 5.2 cm

Blown, naturalistic shaped flamework pear, shaded from yellow to warm pink,
with a yellow stem and green calyx; fused onto a clear almost circular disk.

Museum purchase.
974.310.1

Rose Magnum

American, Mount Washington Glass Company, New Bedford, Massachusetts, 1870–1890
D 9.1 cm, H 5.8 cm

Flamework rose with pink petals and a yellow and aventurine centre, a yellow bud,
a white bud, a stem, and green leaves.

Gift of Alice Baldwin Hall. Certified by the Canadian Cultural Property Export
Review Board under the terms of the Cultural Property Export and Import Act.
981.19.103

Exhibition Paperweight

American, 1893
H 2.2 cm, W 6.7 cm, L 10.5 cm

Clear machine-moulded rectangle with a coloured chromolithograph paper print, captioned "LIBBEY GLASS COMPANY'S FACTORY/WORLD'S COLUMBIAN EXPOSITION 1893," glued to the underside and further backed with maroon "lizard skin" impressed paper.

This acquisition was made possible with the generous support of the J. A. Howson Brocklebank Fund.

989.256.6

Promotional Paperweight

American, 1890s–1920s
H 3.6 cm, W 7.3 cm, L 10.5 cm

Clear machine-moulded contemporary milk-bottle shape; with an enamel photographic illustration of the Owens Automatic Gathering and Blowing Machine and the words "COMPLIMENTS OF THE OWENS BOTTLE MACHINE CO TOLEDO O USA" backed with a thin layer of white enamel.

Gift of Mr. David Roberts.
991.154.9

Photographic Paperweight

American, 1880s–1890s
D 7.6 cm, H 3.3 cm

Clear machine-moulded half sphere with an albumen photograph entitled
"Little Dorothy Barker with the Family Pet Bolivar"
glued to the underside.

Gift of Alice Baldwin Hall. Certified by the Canadian Cultural Property Export
Review Board under the terms of the Cultural Property Export and Import Act.
981.19.234

Millville Rose

American, Whitall Tatum Company, Millville, New Jersey, 1900–1930
D 8.7 cm, H 8.7 cm

Large crimped multi-petalled red rose with four green sepals on a low pedestal;
partial remains of pontil mark.

Gift of Alice Baldwin Hall. Certified by the Canadian Cultural Property Export
Review Board under the terms of the Cultural Property Export and Import Act.
981.19.142

Personal Paperweight

American, 1920s–1930s
D 9.2 cm, H 8 cm

Multi-coloured twisted angled canes (reminiscent of movie-theatre signs) surround a cane supporting the name "Mrs. Reiners" within a red and yellow arrow on either side, suspended above a central cushion of blue chips and four rising multi-coloured air bubbles.

Gift of Alice Baldwin Hall. Certified by the Canadian Cultural Property Export Review Board under the terms of the Cultural Property Export and Import Act.

981.19.149

Canada

Promotional Paperweight

Canadian or American, about 1900–1910
H 2.1 cm, W 6.6 cm, L 10.4 cm

Clear machine-moulded rectangle, backed with a thin blue glass acid-etched flashing
and the words "J. H. FARR & CO./MANUFACTURERS
OF FINE VARNISHES/TORONTO" and "BRAND" in a maple leaf.

Gift of Mr. David Roberts.
991.154.10

Personal Paperweight

Canadian or American, about 1900
D 8.1 cm, H 6.4 cm

Thin white glass rectangle printed in enamel with the words
"J. G. Potter. Esq. Vankleek Hill, Ont."
suspended on a cushion of rose, pale pink, and white chips;
partial pontil mark remains. (Vankleek Hill is near Ottawa, Ontario.)

This acquisition was made possible with the generous support of
the J. A. Howson Brocklebank Fund.

2005.54.1

Personal Paperweight

Canadian, Burlington Glass Works, about 1900
D 8.4 cm, H 6.2 cm

Pink five-petalled lily supported by a central rising air bubble, above two thin white glass
strips with the words in blue "E. MINOR, ST. THOMAS, ONT." suspended above
a cushion of white, red, green, yellow, and blue chips; partial remains of pontil mark.
(St. Thomas is south of London, Ontario.)

The Edith Chown Pierce & Gerald Stevens Collection of Early Canadian Glass.
960.195.19

Promotional Paperweight

Canadian, Sydenham (Dominion) Glass Company Limited,
Wallaceburg, Ontario, about 1900
D 8.2 cm, H 7.1 cm

Thin white glass strip with the words in blue "SYDENHAM GLASS CO." suspended
above four rising air bubbles and a cushion of white, pink, red, blue, yellow, and
pale green chips; partial remains of pontil mark.

The John and Mary Yaremko Collection of Canadian Glass. Certified by
the Canadian Cultural Property Export Review Board under the terms of
the Cultural Property Export and Import Act.

981.163.66

Promotional Paperweight

Canadian, or American, 1900–1920
H 2.8 cm, W 6.8 cm, L 10.6 cm

Clear machine-moulded rectangle, backed with a silvered paper print.

The John and Mary Yaremko Collection of Canadian Glass. Certified by
the Canadian Cultural Property Export Review Board under the terms of
the Cultural Property Export and Import Act.

981.43.902

Tourist Paperweight

Canadian or American, 1900–1920
H 2.6 cm, W 8.3 cm, L 8.3 cm

Clear machine-moulded square, backed with a circular handcoloured photographic
paper print of a large sandstone building with a clock tower and the words
"CITY HALL, TORONTO." [1]

The John and Mary Yaremko Collection of Canadian Glass. Certified by
the Canadian Cultural Property Export Review Board under the terms of
the Cultural Property Export and Import Act.

981.43.904

---

[1] This building at the northeast corner of Queen and Bay streets is now referred to by
Torontonians as Old City Hall. It was designed by architect E. J. Lennox (1854–1933) and
erected in 1899.

See page 79.

English and Scottish Paperweights 1845–1960

Until the 1850s, the only English competition for the French paperweights were the sulphides by Apsley Pellatt, Falcon Glassworks, Southwark, London, and the large elaborate cane paperweights by George Bacchus and Son (later Sons) of Birmingham. Unlike the French paperweights, many Bacchus paperweights were magnum size with low domes and numerous coloured transparent canes.

An English variation of the paperweight was the much larger bottle-green glass "doorstop" paperweight with numerous controlled air bubbles or silver-foil flowers, a tradition begun in the 1800s. Doorstops were made by John Kilner & Sons of Wakefield, Yorkshire, and later by many other unidentified factories.

By the 1920s, several English glass factories were producing paperweights and related novelties such as inkwells. The Alfred Arculus Glassworks of Birmingham made paperweights, as did John Walsh Walsh, also of Birmingham, and James Powell and Sons of Whitefriars in London.

In Scotland, in the second half of the 20th century a number of factories continued the tradition of making both millefiori and flamework paperweights. Paul Ysart revived the art of handmade paperweights. Born in Barcelona, Ysart emigrated to Scotland and worked at the John Moncrieff

Glassworks in Perth. A skilled craftsman, he could produce both caned paper-weights and flamework paperweights with the same high quality. His work displays an element of fun. Many of his paperweights can be identified by his "PY" initial cane.

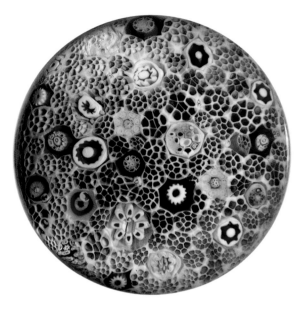

Carpet Magnum

English, George Bacchus and Son, Birmingham, 1845-1855
D 8.7 cm, H 6.3 cm

Spaced millefiori canes and red-lined canes randomly placed with numerous
white mauve-lined "honeycomb" canes.

Gift of Alice Baldwin Hall. Certified by the Canadian Cultural Property Export
Review Board under the terms of the Cultural Property Export and Import Act.
981.19.136

Mushroom with Torsade Magnum

English, George Bacchus and Son, Birmingham, 1845–1850
D 10 cm, H 6.3 cm

Four concentric rings of hollow canes, the inner two red-lined with crimped white tubular
canes, surrounding a central red-lined cane, and surrounded by hollow white canes;
encircled with a pink and white spiral torsade.

Gift of Alice Baldwin Hall. Certified by the Canadian Cultural Property Export
Review Board under the terms of the Cultural Property Export and Import Act.
981.19.102

Concentric Carpet Magnum

English, John Walsh Walsh, Birmingham, 1930s
D 10.7 cm, H 6.5 cm

Concentric carpet with seven rings around an eight-pointed "star,"
the white (third) ring from centre with the red numbers "7/6" in each cane;
fixed in a circular varnished oak frame.

This acquisition was made possible with the generous support of
the J. A. Howson Brocklebank Fund.

2004.82.3

Doorstop

English, 1850s
D 9.6 cm, H 15.8 cm

Green glass with three rows of three silver-foil flowers each rising on an
air bubble from a flower pot made of numerous minute tiny bubbles;
remains of pontil mark.

Gift of Alice Baldwin Hall. Certified by the Canadian Cultural Property Export
Review Board under the terms of the Cultural Property Export and Import Act.
981.19.157

Three Mice

Scottish, Paul Ysart (1904–1991), 1950s
D 6.8 cm, H 5.7 cm

Three flamework mice with two yellow corn kernels on a blackish purple ground with
numerous tiny air bubbles; beside one mouse a white green-edged cane
with the pink initials "PY"; the base with a round white and turquoise sticker with
an interlocking "PY" and "Made in Scotland."

This acquisition was made possible with the generous support of
the J. A. Howson Brocklebank Fund.

987.52.5

Dragonfly

Scottish, Paul Ysart, 1950–1960
D 7.4 cm, H 5.7 cm

Turquoise flamework dragonfly with black-spotted body, red eyes, and beige wings,
set on a deep blue ground with an orange-centred cane on either side of the body,
surrounded by a ring of pale-blue-edged canes; remains of pontil mark.

Gift of Alice Baldwin Hall. Certified by the Canadian Cultural Property Export
Review Board under the terms of the Cultural Property Export and Import Act.

981.19.112

Red Fish

Scottish, Paul Ysart, 1950–1960
D 7.1 cm, H 4.4 cm

Profile of a fish with a rose-striped flamework body, with vermilion mouth and fins,
and yellow and black eye, set on a deep blue ground encircled by a ring of alternating
pink and green canes including a white cane with pink initials "PY."

Gift of Alice Baldwin Hall. Certified by the Canadian Cultural Property Export
Review Board under the terms of the Cultural Property Export and Import Act.
981.19.114

See page 90.

Central and Northern European Paperweights, Chinese Paperweights, 1845–1970

Central European paperweights developed from two distinct traditions; one was the influence of Venetian and French glass and the other was based on local decorating traditions.

Venice was famous in the early 19th century for coloured glass pastes and "Venetian"-style beads in the manufacture of jewellery, so the technical prerequisites for making millefiori canes were already in place. The Silesian glass house Hoffnungsthal, owned by the Preussler family, produced objects incorporating millefiori as early as 1833 and displayed a selection of cutlery handles and door and furniture knobs at the Exhibition of Industry in Mainz in 1842. The Preusslers were well known as glassmakers and decorators since the 17th century. Through family connections and managers, they opened the Josephine Glassworks in 1841, which probably produced the millefiori paperweights with the "j 1848" canes. Other factories also produced paperweights but it is not known if they made their own canes or purchased them.[1]

From the 17th century onwards, Bohemia was also famous for its local glass-cutting and decorating techniques. And although the cutters had to be skilled, the production of a paperweight by this method was simpler, because the decoration was on the surface rather than inside. To make the cutting

---

1 See Michael Kovacek, *Paperweights* (Vienna: Glass Gallery Michael Kovacek, 1987), 119–121.

more obvious, many paperweights have a very thin layer or flashing of glass or a surface colour that was chemically induced.

During the early 20th century, paperweights continued to be produced by only a few continental factories. By the 1950s, however, there was a renewed interest in their manufacture. Italian paperweights produced in the 1950s and 1960s were the most adventuresome in exploring new shapes and ways of highlighting Italy's tradition of millefiori.

Scandinavia had no such history or tradition in glass paperweight-making, and the Italian and French millefiori paperweights seem to have had no influence on their glass. A number of factories, especially in Sweden, had begun to produce paperweights by the 1950s. Scandinavian paperweights are markedly different from those of other countries. Many are colourless and cube-shaped, spherical, or cylindrical in form, with controlled patterns of air bubbles.

The Chinese, who also had no history or tradition in glass paperweight-making, began making paperweights in the 1930s. At first they relied heavily on the Classic French paperweights for inspiration because they were marketing paperweights to Europe and North America. China also produced paperweights similar in appearance to those of the New England Glass Company. Chinese paperweights, however, are made of non-lead glass, which is very cloudy and does not have the clarity of either French or American lead glass.

Engraved Bouquet of Lily-of-the-Valley

Bohemian, 1855–1875
D 8.7 cm, H 5.1 cm

Engraved amber flashing with two stems of lily-of-the-valley and small ferns within
a stylized wreath of paired laurel leaves and berries; with six large circular printies
and one large top printie.

This acquisition was made possible with the generous support of
the J. A. Howson Brocklebank Fund.

989.132.1

Spiral

Italian, Murano, 1950–1965
D 7.8 cm, H 8.6 cm

Clear rounded cone shape with a double spiral of white filigree, the central canes flashed with pink; the base acid-etched in script: "Venini, Murano, Italia."

Gift of Alice Baldwin Hall. Certified by the Canadian Cultural Property Export Review Board under the terms of the Cultural Property Export and Import Act.

981.19.188

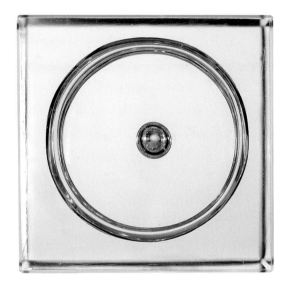

Cube

Sweden, Orrefors, 1960-1970
H 5.1 cm, W 5.2 cm, L 5.2 cm

Clear with a suspended central air bubble and an uneven air-bubble ring;
machine-engraved in script: "orrefors B A 3787"; printed red shield-shaped sticker:
"ORREFORS, SWEDEN."

Gift of Alice Baldwin Hall. Certified by the Canadian Cultural Property Export
Review Board under the terms of the Cultural Property Export and Import Act.
981.19.192

Floral Paperweight

Chinese, 1930s
D 7.1 cm, H 5 cm

Central orange and yellow cane surrounded by six orange petals, six larger yellow petals, and three sepals, on a green stem with two green leaves and one bud.

Gift of Dr. Peter Kaellgren.

975.322

See page 105.

Recent North American Paperweights
1950–Present

United States

The renaissance in American glass paperweights began in the 1950s with the work of Charles Kaziun. He was inspired by the Classic paperweights of the 19th century and the rose paperweights of the Whitall Tatum Company of Millville, New Jersey.

The development of equipment that was smaller and easier to use allowed glass artists to experiment by trial and error. While many of the recent artists have been inspired by the earlier paperweights, they do not imitate them as the late-19th-century and early-20th-century glassmakers did.

Most American paperweight-makers today specialize in flamework, although working with prepared canes has become more popular. Many artists are now pushing the boundaries of paperweight size and technology.

Paul J. Stankard is one of the best and most innovative American glassmakers today, redefining what we think of as a paperweight. His bouquets, "botanicals," and "environmentals" test the viewer's powers of observation. A master of the art of flamework, he has successfully included tiny "earth spirits" (human forms) within the roots of his plants. Recently, he has added word canes to the plant forms.

Taking the paperweight into the realm of sculpture, Stankard has achieved the fusion of numerous paperweights and even combined his work with the works of other glass artists. His latest venture has been ball paperweights that mystify and delight because they have no defined base.

In the world of paperweights, flamework birds, animals, and reptiles are rarer than the individual flowers and floral bouquets, which have remained popular with makers and buyers since they first appeared in France in the 1840s. Roland "Rick" Ayotte (b. 1944), also American, was one of the few artists specializing in bird subjects in the 1970s and 1980s. Although he has moved on to other subjects, his early birds still fascinate collectors.

Canada

In Canada, few glassmakers focus entirely on paperweights, and we have fewer paperweight artists who can compete internationally. The relatively smaller population makes it less easy to earn a living specializing in paperweights. Still, Canada does have some very fine artists who deserve recognition for their excellence.

Special mention must be made of the late John Gooderham of Sault Ste. Marie, Ontario, who is recognized as producing "the smallest yet most perfect" double-overlay paperweight that has ever been made.

United States

Garland of Forget-me-nots

American, Melissa Ayotte (b. 1977), 2004
D 8 cm, H 5.4 cm

Flamework, open garland of blue and pink buds, partially opened flowers, and fully opened flowers; with yellowish green leaves and tendrils; the underside with a white blue-edged cane with "MA"; engraved near base: "M. Ayotte 2004."

This acquisition was made possible with the generous support of the J. A. Howson Brocklebank Fund.

2005.52.17

Four Turtles in a Pond

American, Rick Ayotte (b. 1944), 2003
D 11.5 cm, H 7.7 cm

Three flamework turtles swimming at different levels in a pond, and one floating on a piece of wood near a pink water-lily; the pond's sand bottom is covered with "living" green plants and clams and rotting leaf, fruit, and stems; engraved on base: "Rick Ayotte 1 of 1 2003."

This acquisition was made possible with the generous support of the J. A. Howson Brocklebank Fund.

2003.44.1

Antique Bouquet

American, Ray Banford (1918–2003) and Bob Banford (b. 1951), 1980s
D 8.3 cm, H 6.5 cm

Stylized flamework bouquet with a pink rose, a red flower with two rows of six red
petals, a purple and yellow pansy with a white centre cane with a purple flower,
a yellow "wheatflower," one red bud, one yellow bud, numerous green stems
and green leaves; at bottom of bouquet a white cane with a black "B"
and a blue-edged cane with a mauve "B"; diamond-cut base.

This acquisition was made possible with the generous support of
the J. A. Howson Brocklebank Fund.

2005.52.13

Summer Harvest

American, Jim D'Onofrio (b. 1951), 1992
D 8.8 cm, H 6.8 cm

Naturalistic white and black flamework rabbit sitting on a green, brown, and white sand
ground, surrounded by a bundle of carrots, a corn cob, an onion, a tomato, a turnip,
two gourds, and an eggplant; engraved in script on side: "Jim Donofrio 01 1244."

This acquisition was made possible with the generous support of
the J. A. Howson Brocklebank Fund.

2005.52.12

Pedestal with Red Tulip

American, Charles Kaziun (1919–1992), 1950s
D of foot 6.2 cm, H 8.2 cm

Red flamework tulip with two rows of three red pink-edged petals and three black stamens surrounding a yellow stigma, with three green "sepals" (although tulips do not have sepals); centred on the underside, a white cane with a blue "K" surrounded by seven tiny orange-centred yellow canes; set upon a clear glass pedestal.

Gift of Alice Baldwin Hall. Certified by the Canadian Cultural Property Export Review Board under the terms of the Cultural Property Export and Import Act.
981.19.121

Strawberries

American, James Kontes, 1980s
D 7.5 cm, H 5.2 cm

One white flamework ribbed flower with a yellow star cane centre, one white bud, and three red strawberries with green stems and three green leaves, on scrambled white filigree encircled by a white twisted cane; deep blue ground; white cane near base with a purple connected "JK" surrounded by yellow stars.

Bequest of J. A. Howson Brocklebank. Certified by the Canadian Cultural Property Export Review Board under the terms of the Cultural Property Export and Import Act.

984.266.50

Bouquet

American, Johne Parsley (b. 1916), 1989
D 6.7 cm, H 5.5 cm

Three pink flamework dogwood flowers, each with four pink bracts surrounding
a cluster of tiny yellow flowers; with a spike of vermilion and a spike of yellow knotweed,
and three yellow-green striped trifoliate leaves; blue ground; white green-edged cane
with "P"; engraved on edge: "JP-1989."

This acquisition was made possible with the generous support of
the J. A. Howson Brocklebank Fund.

989.134.4

Megaplanet

American, Josh Simpson (b. 1949), 1989
D 15.9 cm, H 15.9 cm

A large spherical deep blue-black and cream-coloured "ocean" with mottled brown
and beige "landmasses" accentuated with gold leaf highlights and groupings of raised
millefiori cane "mountains" set under numerous small patterned and trailing
air bubbles; the surface with two groupings of scrambled canes; engraved in
flourishing script on base: "Simpson, 1989 4.3."

This acquisition was made possible with the generous support of
the J. A. Howson Brocklebank Fund.

990.91.1

Marbled Reed Frog with Bamboo

American, Gordon Smith (b. 1959), 2004
D 8.1 cm, H 5.7 cm

Naturalistic mauve and purple flamework marbled reed frog, on a white, brown, and beige chip ground with decaying bamboo, three pale five-petalled green aquatic (buttercup family) flowers, and a palm branch; engraved on side at base: "GS 04–11."

This acquisition was made possible with the generous support of the J. A. Howson Brocklebank Fund.

2006.43.1

Pineland Pickerel-Weed Botanical with Blueberries,
Ants, Damselfly, and Mask

American, Paul Joseph Stankard (b. 1943), 2001
H 13.8 cm, W 7 cm

Yellow flamework pineland pickerel-weed and blueberries above a rust-red "mask" backed
with roots and a "root" person (plant spirit), two white orange–edged word canes that spell
"SEEDS" at bottom; with two crawling ants and a hovering damselfly; engraved near base:
"Paul J. Stankard T7 2001."

This acquisition was made possible with the generous support of
the J. A. Howson Brocklebank Fund.

2001.121.1

Bouquet

American, Debby Tarsitano (b. 1955), 1989
D 9.1 cm, H 6 cm

A central grouping of three red and pink five-petalled flamework flowers surrounded
by three blue five-petalled flowers and three buds, two white striped five-petalled flowers
with pink central petals, and three yellow "flowers," all with yellow centres, numerous
green leaves, and brown stems tied at base; star-cut base.

This acquisition was made possible with the generous support of
the J. A. Howson Brocklebank Fund.

989.134.2

Strawberries

American, Delmo Tarsitano (1921–1991), 1980s
D 7.8 cm, H 5.7 cm

Flamework, three white strawberry blossoms with yellow centres,
three red strawberries, with green stems, and eight green leaves; the underside
with two white blue-edged canes with illegible letters.

This acquisition was made possible with the generous support of
the J. A. Howson Brocklebank Fund.

2005.52.9

Salamander Magnum

American, Victor Trabucco (b. 1949), 2001
D 12.5 cm, H 10.6 cm

Naturalistic green-scaled flamework salamander on a ground of rust, brown,
and white sand with a pink flower with spiralling green and brown striped leaves;
the underside with a central white cane with mauve initials "VT";
engraved on base: "Trabucco 2001."

This acquisition was made possible with the generous support of
the J. A. Howson Brocklebank Fund.

2001.51.1.1

Canada

Gold Veil

Canadian, Ontario, Mark Armstrong (b. 1965), 1999
D 7 cm, H 12.1 cm

A purple "cushion" with a central air bubble surrounded by rising air bubbles;
under gold leaf; engraved on base: "Mark Armstrong."

Gift of Mark Armstrong.
2000.90.2

Miniature Double Overlay with Printies

Canadian, Ontario, John Gooderham (1930–2007), 1985
D 1.4 cm, H 0.8 cm

A red and white overlay with a central gold-foil flower and
a hovering butterfly on a deep blue ground.

This acquisition was made possible with the generous support of
the J. A. Howson Brocklebank Fund.

986.200.3

Pink Stock Flowers

Canadian, British Columbia, Robert Held (b. 1943), 2006
D 9.3 cm, H 13.7 cm

A large egg-shaped paperweight with two similar plants on opposite sides, each with
five pink- and rose-striped flowers with small circular iridescent centres placed
above white and green "whiplashed" striped leaves; tomato-red ground;
engraved on base: "R. Held Art Glass"; on base, gold-coloured oval sticker with
black lettering: "ROBERT HELD/HAND MADE/IN CANADA/ART GLASS."

This acquisition was made possible with the generous support of
the J. A. Howson Brocklebank Fund.

2007.14.1

Galaxy

Canadian, Ontario, Toan Klein (b. 1949), 1981
D 7.6 cm, H 6.4 cm

A deep blue-black swirl with iridescent white chips below gold leaf;
engraved at edge of base: "Toan 1981."

Gift of Ms. Nancy Shanoff.
982.96.1

Pink Trillium

Canadian, Ontario, Andrew Kuntz (b. 1956), 1998
H 12 cm, W 12 cm

Irregular fan shape with large flamework three-petalled rose-coloured trillium with
large central air bubble, on a mottled white, black, and green "moss"-covered rock;
engraved on side of base: "Andrew Kuntz 1998."

Gift of Arthur Smith in honour of Al and Peggy (MacKay) Rogers.
2006.109.1

Painted Paperweight

Canadian, Mark Lewis (b. 1958), 2005
D 8.5 cm, H 4.3 cm

Low circular clear glass dome over a painted abstract centre in yellow, blue,
grey, and red, decorated with black circles and "V"s and white crosses;
engraved on base: "Mark Lewis 05."

This acquisition was made possible with the generous support of
the J. A. Howson Brocklebank Fund.

2007.14.2

Bubble Weight

Canadian, New Brunswick, Jon Sawyer (b. 1955), 1993
D 6.8 cm, H 6.2 cm

Two central air bubbles above two greenish blue swirls,
each within a beige air-bubble net; engraved on base: "Sawyer 93."

Gift of Arthur Smith in honour of Al and Peggy (Mackay) Rogers.
2006.109.2

Hot-Formed and Laminated Paperweight

Canadian, Ontario, Karl Schantz (b. 1944), 1987
D 7.4 cm, H 6.9 cm

Black sphere with a circle of laminated stripes of mauve, blue, green,
yellow, orange, and red; engraved on base: "Karl Schantz, 1987."

This acquisition was made possible with the generous support of
the J. A. Howson Brocklebank Fund.

988.17.1

Mutant Brain

Canadian, Ontario, Virginia Wilson Toccalino (b. 1955) and Tony Toccalino (b. 1952), 2006
D 8.2 cm, H 7 cm

A central air bubble surrounded by a black-edged sky-blue ribbon backed in yellow
and brown and randomly twisted with a wide ribbon of yellow filigree;
engraved on edge at base: "Virginia Wilson Toccalino."

This acquisition was made possible with the generous support of
the J. A. Howson Brocklebank Fund.

2006.59.5

Kovacek, Michael. *Paperweights.* Vienna: Glass Gallery Michael Kovacek, 1987.

Kulles, George N. *Identifying Antique Paperweights: Lampwork.* Santa Cruz, CA: Paperweight Press, 1987.

__. *Identifying Antique Paperweights: Millefiori.* Santa Cruz, CA: Paperweight Press, 1987.

Newell, Clarence A. *Old Glass Paperweights of Southern New Jersey.* Phoenix, AZ: Papier Presse, 1989.

Newman, Harold. *An Illustrated Dictionary of Glass.* London: Thames and Hudson, 1977.

Pellatt, Apsley. *Memoir on the Origin, Progress, and Improvement of Glass Manufactures: Including an Account of the Patent Crystallo Ceramie, or, Glass Incrustations.* London: B. J. Holdsworth, 1821.

Sarpellon, Giovanni. *Miniature Masterpieces: Mosaic Glass 1838–1924.* Munich and New York: Prestel, 1995.

Schoolley-West, R. F. *Stamps.* London: British Library, 1987.

Selman, Lawrence H. *The Art of the Paperweight.* Santa Cruz, CA: Paperweight Press, 1988.

Stevens, Gerald. *Canadian Glass, c. 1825–1925.* Toronto: Ryerson Press, 1967.

Young, John H. *Our Deportment or the Manners, Conduct and Dress of the Most Refined Society; Including Forms for Letters, Invitations, Etc., Etc. Also, Valuable Suggestions on Home Culture and Training.* Detroit and St. Louis: F. B. Dickerson & Co., rev. ed., 1882.

Bibliography

Bruhn, Jutta-Annette. *Designs in Miniature: The Story of Mosaic Glass.* Corning, NY: Corning Museum of Glass, 1995.

Casper, Geraldine J. *Glass Paperweights in the Art Institute of Chicago.* Chicago: Art Institute of Chicago, 1991.

Dietz, Ulysses Grant. *Paul J Stankard: Homage to Nature.* New York: Harry N. Abrams, 1996.

Hall, Robert G. *English Paperweights.* Atglen, PA: Schiffer Publishing, 1998.
___. *Scottish Paperweights.* Atglen, PA: Schiffer Publishing, 1999.
___. *World Paperweights: Millefiori & Lampwork.* Atglen, PA: Schiffer Publishing, 2001.
Hawley, John D. *The Glass Menagerie.* Santa Cruz, CA: Paperweight Press, 1995.
___. *The Art of the Paperweight: The Boston & Sandwich and New England Glass Companies.* Santa Cruz, CA: Paperweight Press, 1997.
Hollister, Paul. *Paperweights from the Henry Melville Fuller Collection.* Manchester, NH: Currier Gallery of Art, 1993.
Hollister, Paul, Jr. *The Encyclopedia of Glass Paperweights.* New York: Bramhall House, 1969.
Holmes, Janet. *Patterns in Light: The John and Mary Yaremko Glass Collection.* Toronto: Royal Ontario Museum, 1987.

Ingold, Gérard. *The Art of the Paperweight: Saint Louis.* Santa Cruz, CA: Paperweight Press, 1981.

Jargstorf, Sibylle. *Paperweights.* West Chester, PA: Schiffer Publishing, 1991.
Jokelson, Paul. *Sulphides: The Art of Cameo Incrustation.* New York: Galahad Books, 1968.
Jokelson, Paul, and Dena K. Tarshis. *Cameo Incrustation: The Great Sulphide Show.* Santa Cruz, CA: Paperweight Press, 1988.